THE MCCROSKEY FAMILY HISTORY

Scotland / Ireland To Virginia & East Tennessee

By Katherine Fletcher

McCROSKEY FAMILY HISTORY

This book is about the McCroskey Family History. My son is a McCroskey and my future grandchildren will be also.

Discovering our own family history is so important for so many reasons. It gives us a sense of where we came from and who we are. It reminds us how strong our ancestors were and how we can be strong and brave too. We are the pieces of all who came before us.

Our ancestors lived remarkable lives and were brave enough to leave their homelands in foreign countries and come to America to start over. They settled this country, raised families, went through wars, disease and constant change. They were remarkable people in a new land called America and paved the way for many of the things we hold dear – constitutional rights, freedom of religion and speech, education, morals, values, attitudes and belief systems. We inherited all of these from our various ancestors.

We are also a true mix of many different races, cultures and religions. Our ancestors did come from foreign countries all over the world. Once they got to America they married people from different backgrounds, races. They intermixed with the Native Indians, had children with their slaves and intertwined many different races, cultures. America is truly a "melting pot".

DEDICATION

This book is dedicated to all my son's family members and the new descendants to come.

McCroskey

McCROSKEY FAMILY HISTORY

The name McCroskey started on the rugged Scottish west coast in a place called Hebrides islands in the ancient Kalriadan kingdom. It was a nickname for a person with blond hair.   They were later found in Argyllshire where they held a family seat from very ancient times, before the Norman Conquest (1066 AD).

On the Scottish side there are many variations of spelling to the McCroskey name including Crone, Cron, Cronie. Cron was the Gaelic word for "saffron, yellow colored".

  On the Irish side, the McCroskey's originate from Wigtown, Scotland Scotch-Irish and were originally fom Antrim, Ireland.   Other name spinoffs are McCloskey, McCosqry, McCroskery, McClosky,.   The original spelling was Cosgrave and the Mc was added in later.

AMERICAN MIGRATION

Many other immigrants followed from Scotland and Ireland and settled in the New World of America.   Most of the immigrants came in the 1700-1800's.

This branch of McCroskey's came from Augusta County, Virginia and are descendants of Samuel McCroskey, minister of Accomac County, VA in the 17th century.   The McCroskey's were Presbyterians. This line continues to a Revolutionary War soldier and is connected to General Sam Houston of Texas.

The McCroskey families, along with other well-recognized families, helped to pave the way for the early settlements in Washington, Jefferson, Sevier, Blount, and Monroe Counties. The McCroskey, Montgomery, McCray, Nodding, Grant, Gallaher, Cunningham, Houston, Barrett, Mayo, Eagleton, Gilbreath, and Hope families make up a modern day "Who's Who in History." A McCroskey Family Tree shows family connections to all of these families mentioned as well as others that we read about in TN History.

These families had close ties to the Presbyterian Church and played an important part in its organization in America. They served their country well with many taking part in a number of military campaigns.

John Blair McCroskey served in the Revolutionary War, fought at King's Mountain and in several Indian skirmishes (Pension # S2781). His wife was Ann Montgomery. Two of his sons, John McCroskey and Samuel McCroskey settled in Fork Creek Valley, east of Sweetwater, in Monroe Co., TN.

John McCroskey was the first High Sheriff (1820 – 1830) in Monroe Co. and his brother, Samuel was the first Postmaster in Morganton and both held a number of political offices for many years. Their descendants became lawyers, educators, ministers, owners of various businesses, farmers, as well as serving in a number of political positions. Many of their descendants settled into other areas of TN as well as California and Washington State." (Text by Dede Harrill & Joy Locke)

FIRST FIVE
GENERATIONS

William McCroskey
B: 26 Nov 1848 , Tennessee, USA
M: 21 Dec 1884
D: 7 Feb 1900

David McCroskey
B: 23 Feb 1805 , Tennessee, USA
D: 7 Aug 1885 Tennessee, USA

Elizabeth Clack Rogers
B: 15 Aug 1805 , Tennessee, USA
D: 8 Dec 1864 , Tennessee, USA

Charles Jennings McCroskey
B: 22 Dec 1897 Sevierville, TN
M:
D: 1 Jan 1988 Knoxville, TN

Alice Householder
B: 27 Jan 1868 Tennessee, USA
M: 21 Dec 1884
D: 23 Nov 1983 , Virginia, USA

William M Householder
B: 18 Jan 1843 Tennessee, USA
D: 24 Jun 1925 Tennessee, USA

Rebecca Jane Whittle
B: 17 Mar 1849 Tennessee, USA
D: 10 Mar 1935 Tennessee, USA

Shadrick Beuford McCroskey
B: 1929
M:
D:

Sam McMurray
B: 15 Oct 1871 , Tennessee, USA
M:
D: 14 Aug 1942 Tennessee, USA

Bartley Russell MCMURRAY
B: 8 May 1831 , Tennessee, USA
D: 28 Dec 1910 , Tennessee, USA

Mary Elizabeth HOUSEHOLDER
B: 15 Dec 1844
D: 11 Feb 1935 , Tennessee, USA

Johnnie Kate McMurray
B: 1904 , Blount, Tennessee, USA
M:
D: 1991 Knoxville, Tennessee

Minnie Gilbert
B: Mar 1885 , Tennessee, USA
M:
D:

James D GILBERT
B: Jan 1852 , , Tennessee, USA
D:

Martha J
B: Mar 1858 , , Tennessee, USA
D:

James Dennis McCroskey
B: 18 August 1956
M:

<h1 style="text-align:center">GENERATION ONE:</h1>

James Dennis McCroskey and Katherine Fletcher

Children: Cody Jennings McCroskey
Dennis's child with first wife Lisa is Jessica McCroskey

<h1 style="text-align:center">GENERATION TWO:</h1>

Shadrick Beuford McCroskey and Shirley Parton McCroskey
1929 to 2009

Shadrick was born in Seymour, Tennessee and also died there.
Shadrick (Bud) was a light hearted funny guy.   He was kind and
gently and always had a story to tell.   He ran a tavern in Seymour
called McCroskey's Tavern and worked at Sears for many years.
Bud also served in the U.S. Navy from 1946-1948.
Shirley Parton was born in 1936 in Sevierville, TN. Her parents are
Albert C. Parton and Marie Florence Gunnels. Her grandparents
were part Mohawk and Cherokee.

Bud and Shirley's Children are:

Charles McCroskey –
James Dennis McCroskey – children: Jessica and Cody
Shadrick (Rick) McCroskey – children Jake and Charlie

Shadrick Beuford's (BUD) OBITUARY

MCCROSKEY, SHADRICK B. (BUD) - age 80 of Knoxville, passed away on Friday, July 3, 2009. He was a member of Gloria Dei Luthern Church. He served with the U. S. Navy during the World War II era on the USS Leyte CV-32. He was retired from Sears. Preceded in death by parents, Charles Jennings and Johnie Kate McCroskey, brother-in-law, Bill Richards. Survived by wife of 56 years Shirley J. McCroskey; sons and daughters-in-law Charles C. and Kelly, Dennis, Rick and Terry McCroskey; grandchildren, Jessica, Cody, Jake and Charley; great grandchildren, Liam and Ella Blue; brothers and sister-in-law, Ken and Pat McCroskey, Jerry and Mildred McCroskey; sisters and brothers-in-law, Ruth and Bill Odell and Betty Richards; brothers-in-law, J.J. Parton and Tony Catlett; several nieces and nephews

Left to Right: Shadrick Beauford (BUD) with sons Chuck, Rick and Dennis (standing) at their home in Seymour, TN.

Bud and grandsons: Left to Right: Jake, Charlie, Cody

SHIRLEY MCCROSKEY – WIFE OF SHADRICK BEUFORD (BUD)
WITH GRANDSON CODY AND THE THREE LEGGED DOG MISSY

Shadrick (Bud) McCroskey, Shirley Parton McCroskey
And three sons, three grandchildren and two great grandchildren

FLAG FROM SHIP THAT BUD SERVED ON IN NAVY IN WWII

THE SHIP USS LEYTE – WHERE BUD SERVED IN WORLD WAR II

GENERATION THREE

Charles Jennings McCroskey and Johnnie Kate McMurray
(1897-1988)   (1903-1991)

Charles (CJ) was born 1897 in Tennessee and died January 1, 1988 in Seymour, TN.

He was a wonderful man I had the pleasure of knowing briefly when I was married to his grandson, Dennis. He loved to tell stories and sit on the porch and visit with people.   He was very old when I knew him but liked him so much I named by son after him, using Jennings as his middle name.

His first tragedy was the death of his father William when Charles was three years old.

In 1900 he was 2 years old and lived with a large group of McCroskey's and Householders (his grandparents).   His grandparents were farmers.

When he was 12 years old he went to Illinois and worked as a mule skinner. He had a 12 horse team.   During World War II, he joined the Navy at 17 and served on the ship USS Columbia Philadelphia.

He bought first tavern in downtown Knoxville, called Charlie's Tavern and Rainbow Room. There was a tavern in one part and restaurant and dance in the other part.   He also had a 10 room motel called Mccroskey court.

In 1920 the census says he was living with his McMurray family. He was 22, single and living with his brother in law Luther McMurray. Luther married his sister Minnie McCroskey and this is probably how he met Johnnie Kate McMurray his future wife.

According to the 1940 census, Charles (age 42) was working as a watchman for an Irons Works factory Sanford and days. The census states he completed the 7th grade. It also states that in 1939 we only had 13 weeks of work for the whole year.

Charles Jennings and Johnnie McMurray's children were:

Ruth – 1923 married Bill O'Dell
Shadrick Buford (bud) married Shirley Jean Parton –born
February 13, 1929 to July 3, 2009
Ken 1932 to married Patsy King
Betty 1934 married Bill Richards
Jerry 1937 married Mildred

GENERATION FOUR

William Leonidas McCroskey and Tulah Alice Householder

William was born 1848 in Sevierville and died in 1900. He married in 1884 in Sevier County.

Alice was born 1868 in Tennessee and died in 1951 in Knox Co, TN.

Alice's parents were William Madison Householder and Rebecca Jane Whittle. Rebecca Whittles parents are Felix Low Whittle 1826-1909 and Margaret Fox (1828-1896). Both were born and died in Sever County, TN.

The Householder line goes back to Germany 1716 and was spelled Haushalter. The Householder Family has been in the United States since the early 1700s and are from immigrated from Russheim, Germany. The Whittle family was in Amherst, Virginia in the 1700's. This Whittle family has a long and important history around Knoxville, TN.

In 1850, William was living in McMinn County, TN at age 2.
In 1860, age 12 William was living in Sevier County.   In 1884 he
married Telula Alice Householder.

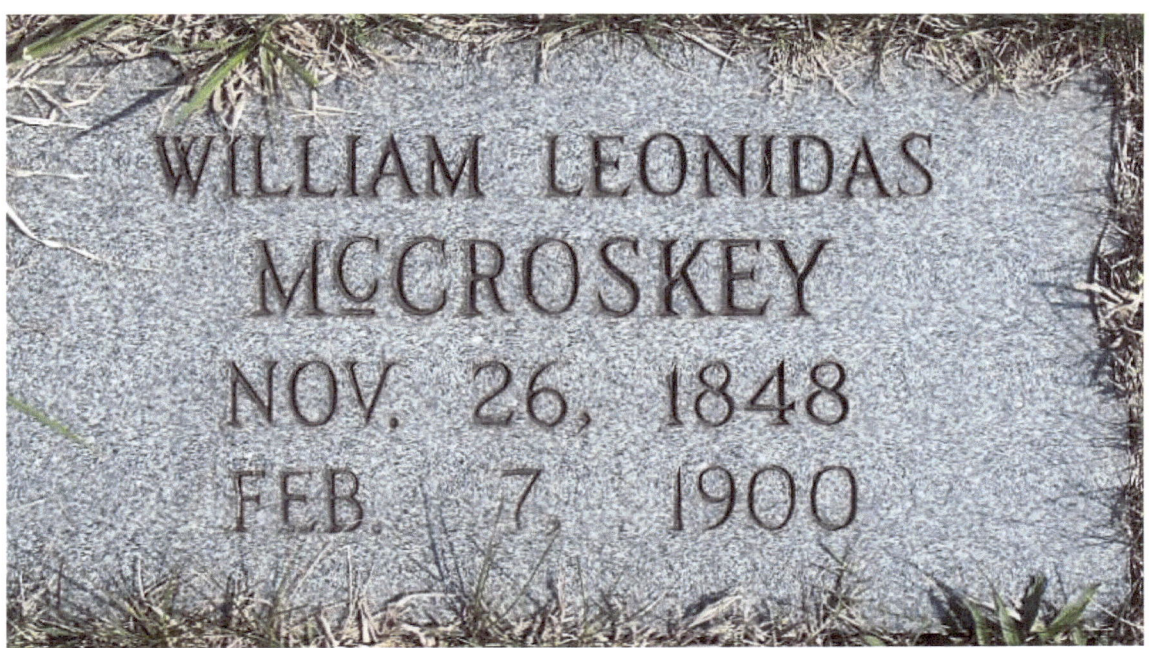

WILLIAM LEONIDAS
McCROSKEY
NOV. 26, 1848
FEB. 7 1900

TULLAH A. HOUSEHOLDER
McCROSKEY
JAN. 27, 1868
OCT. 3, 1951

William and Alice's Children were:

Charles Jennings McCroskey 1897 –1988. married Johnnie Kate McMurray
William Herbert – 1900-married Bebe Asherman – at age 20 he was in Champaign, Illinois.
Bertha Jane – 1890 – married Thomas Owen Turley
Orlando Ernest -1892-1980 married Faye Utter, died in Iowa
Miinie Lee. – 1886-1962 Blount Co, TN married Luther McMurray
Pearl Elizabeth – 1888-1935 Blount Co, TN – she married John C. Clark and J.R. McCammon

Here's a picture of William Householder and Rebecca Jane Whittle, Alice's parents.

William Matt Householder & his sister, Mary Eliz. Householder McMurray

GENERATION FIVE

David McCroskey and Jane, then Elizabeth Clark Rogers, then Harriet Truwitt

David was born 1805 in Sevier County, TN and died in 1885. He also married Harriet Truwitt and had 4 more children. David died in Cleveland Tennessee in 1885 at age 80.

Elizabeth was born 1805 and died in 1846. She was born and died in Sevier Co, Tn. Elizabeth's parents were Rev. Elijah Rogers (1774-1841) Farquier, VA and died in Sevier County, Tennessee. Her mother was Catherine Fairfax Clack (1778-1850). The Rogers side of her family goes back to Dunkirk, VA in 1721 and a death in Buncombe County, NC (Asheville). ** SEE ADDITION TO END OF BOOK WITH STORY ABOUT REV. ELIJAH ROGERS, the famous Baptist preacher.

David and Elizabeth's 10 children:

David Oscar – 1829-1911
Elizabeth – 1831
Spencer C. – 1833
Mary – 1835
James M. – 1839
Sarah M. 1841
Rachel C. 1843-1885 Tennessee married Sylvanus Mathewson Ball
Matilda – 1845-1916
William Leonidas – 1848-1900
Louisa Elizabeth – 1831-1897

David and Harriets children:

Elijah – 1837
Agnes – 1874- married Joseph Elijah Foster
Harriet – 1866-1922 married John Richmond
Andrew – 1868

David McCroskey homestead – Sevierville, TN

James David McCroskey homestead – Sevierville, TN

GENERATION SIX TO TEN

John McCroskey
B: 1680 Antrim, Antrim, , Ireland
M:
D: 1758 Virginia, USA

John McCroskey
B: 1620 Ireland
D:

Louisa
B: 1600 Scotland
D: 1648 Scotland

Samuel McCroskey
B: 1725 , Augusta, Virginia, USA
M: 20 Mar 1753 , Virginia, USA
D: 11 Nov 1797 , Kentucky, USA

Elizabeth Gay
B: 1680 Wigtown, , Scotland
M:
D: 1758 , Virginia, USA

John Gay
B:
D:

Mary Fisher
B:
D:

Alexander McCroskey
B: 1764 , Augusta, Virginia, USA
M:
D: 1780 , , North Carolina, USA

Elizabeth Blair
B: 1725 , Augusta, Virginia, USA
M: 20 Mar 1753 , Virginia, USA
D: 11 Nov 1797 , Virginia, USA

David McCroskey
B: 1780 , Sevier, Tennessee, USA
M:
D: 1 Jul 1826 , Sevier, Tennessee, USA

GENERATION SIX

David McCroskey and Jane _____

David was born around 1780 and died in 1826. David had 300 acres of land on Boyd's Creek in Sevierville, TN (see Land Deed below) Jane ?

David and Jane's children:

David – 1805-1885
William -
John - 1796 to 1872 – lived all his life in Sevier County, Tennessee, died at age 76.

David McCroskey Land Purchase

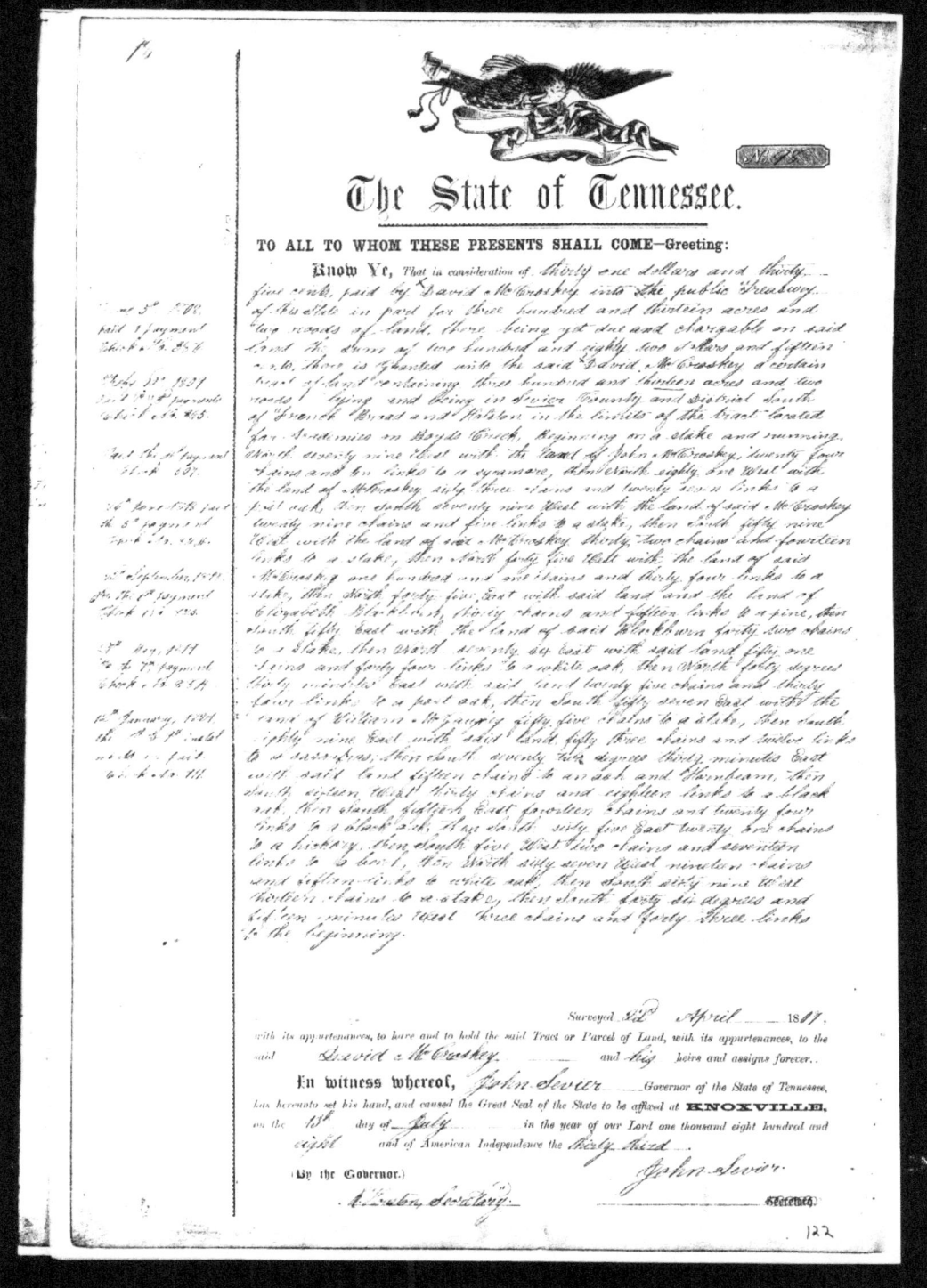

The State of Tennessee.

TO ALL TO WHOM THESE PRESENTS SHALL COME—Greeting:

Know Ye, That in consideration of *thirty one dollars and thirty five cents*, paid by *David McCroskey* into the public Treasury of this State in part for *three hundred and thirteen acres and two roods of land, there being yet due and chargable on said land the sum of two hundred and eighty two dollars and fifteen cents, there is Granted unto the said David McCroskey a certain tract of land containing three hundred and thirteen acres and two roods, lying and being in Sevier County and District South of French Broad and Holston in the limits of the tract located for Academies on Boyds Creek, beginning on a stake and running North seventy nine West with the land of John McCroskey, twenty four chains and ten links to a sycamore, thence South eighty two West with the land of McCroskey sixty three chains and twenty seven links to a post oak, then South seventy nine West with the land of said McCroskey twenty nine chains and five links to a stake, then South fifty nine West with the land of said McCroskey thirty two chains and fourteen links to a stake, then North forty five West with the land of said McCroskey one hundred and one chains and thirty four links to a stake, then North forty four East with said land and the land of Elizabeth Blackburn, thirty chains and fifteen links to a pine, then South fifty East with the land of said Blackburn forty two chains to a stake, then North seventy six East with said land fifty one chains and forty four links to a white oak, then North fifty degrees thirty minutes East with said land twenty five chains and thirty four links to a post oak, then South fifty seven East with the land of William McGaughy fifty five chains to a stake, then South eighty nine East with said land, forty three chains and twelve links to a sassafras, then South seventy two degrees thirty minutes East with said land fifteen chains to an ash and dogwood, then South sixteen West thirty chains and eighteen links to a black oak, then South fifteen East fourteen chains and twenty four links to a black oak, then South sixty five East twenty two chains to a hickory, then South five West five chains and seventeen links to a beech, then North sixty seven West nineteen chains and fifteen links to a white oak, then South sixty nine West thirteen chains to a stake, then South forty six degrees and fifteen minutes West three chains and forty three links to the beginning.*

Surveyed *the 2d* April ___ 18*07*.

with its appurtenances, to have and to hold the said Tract or Parcel of Land, with its appurtenances, to the said *David McCroskey* ___ and *his* heirs and assigns forever.

In witness whereof, *John Sevier* ___ Governor of the State of Tennessee, has hereunto set his hand, and caused the Great Seal of the State to be affixed at **KNOXVILLE,** on the *15th* day of *July* ___ in the year of our Lord one thousand eight hundred and *eight* and of American Independence the *Thirty Third* ___

(By the Governor.)   *John Sevier*

W. Baton, Secretary   Recorded.

(left margin notes)

*June 3d 1808,
raid 1 payment
Check No 854*

*Septr 16th 1801,
raid 2nd payments
Check No 815.*

*Raid the 3d payment
Check 857.*

*16 June 6th paid
the 5th payment
Check No 216.*

*2d September, 1801,
On the 6th payment
Check No 25*

*8th May, 1811
On the 7th payment
Check No 254*

*16th January, 1801
the 8 & 9th raid
with the last
Check No 111*

GENERATION SEVEN

Alexander McCroskey

Alexander McCroskey was born in 1764 in Augusta, Virginia and died in 1780. He was 16 years old.   I cannot find information on his spouse but he had a son David.

David: born 1780 in died in 1826. He married Jane _____

GENERATION EIGHT

Samuel Smith McCroskey and Elizabeth Blair

Samuel McCroskey was born in 1725 in Antrim, Ireland and died in 1797 in Fayette, Kentucky. He moved from Ireland to Rockbridge, VA long before the war. Later he moved to Wythville, VA. In 1754 he bought 440 acres from his father John McCroskey. He married Elizabeth Blair in 1756 in Augusta Co, Virginia.

She must have died or they divorced because in 1788 he sold those 440 acres to a Davis Vance. He remarried and then moved to Kentucky. His descendants are spread out through Kentucky, Texas, Missouri and Tennessee.
He was in the Revolutionary War and if you are related to him you can apply for the sons or daughter of the American Revolution.

Elizabeth Blair was the first wife born in 1725 Virginia and died 1797. He also married Mary Blackwood in Rockbridge, Virginia in 1777.

Old McCroskey homestead of Virginia 1784

Samuel and Elizabeth's children were:

Alexander – 1764 Augusta Co, VA to 1780 – died at age 16 but somehow had a son named David???
Elizabeth – 1766 Augusta Co, VA
Esther 1756 married Joseph Walker
James 1760-1835 Augusta Co, VA. Married Susan Walker (1762-1835)
Robert 1762 Augusta Co, VA
William – 1772 Augusta Co, VA to 1856 Urbana, Ohio. Married Mary Ferris.
John Blair 1757-1843 Timber Ridge, VA to Sevier Co. married Ann Houston Montgomery. Ann Houston is part of the famous Sam Houston family. Revolutionary War soldier in the Battle of Kings Mountain and others.
Alexander MCCROSKEY b: ABT. 1764 in Augusta Co., VA

The DOAKS family is also connected with McCroskey's and Houston's.

Samuel and Mary Blackwood's children:

Ann
David – born 1818 KY
Elijah – born in KY
Levi
Mary Nealy –
Ann Spires -

Samuel – 1757-1843 – it was Samuels son Samuel that went to Sevier Co, TN.   Another one of Samuel's sons was James McCroskey 1760-1835.   He served in the Virginia militia and was standing beside George Washington when Cornwallis handed over sword at Yorktown.   Samuel married Charlotte Taylor in 1772 and also married Elizabeth Bowdoin in 1780.

Sally Blackwood -

TIMBER RIDGE PRESBYTERIAN CHURCH

Scotch Irish settlers began occupying the valley west of the Blue Ridge Mountains in the late 1720's until the entire area was known as the "Irish Tract". Tradition says John Mackey was the first to settle on Timber Ridge, having built his cabin by 1727. Ephriam McDowell was the first to record his land title in 1737.

It was to these hardy pioneers that Rev. John Blair, Minister of Donegal Presbyterian in Pennsylvania, came to organize the "Presbyterian Society" which met in the Timber Grove meeting House in 1746. Blair was a "New Side" minister influenced by the evangelistic pattern of Whitefield.

Matthew Lyle and Ester Blair, his wife, both dedicated Presbyterians, gave a site on their land for the construction of a sanctuary some time after 1737. The first building was a log structure with openings in one of the chinkings on all four sides to provide port-holes in case of Indian attack. The southbound lane of U.S. 11 now passes over the spot near the H. D. Mackey farm where this log church was in use around 1741.

In 1758, Rev. John Brown became the first pastor, serving New Providence as well. The call for his services was signed by 112 men and four women of the two congregations. Among the signers were the great-grandfather (John Houston) and the grandfather (Robert Houston) of General Sam Houston, of Tennessee and Texas fame.

Under the leadership of the Rev. Mr. Brown and a building committee consisting of James McClung and John Lyle, the movement for a new larger building on a new site culminated in the erection of the stone church upon a tract of land purchased from Robert Houston. This building is now the main body of the present structure. A quarry of native limestone close by furnished the stone for the walls and "The Nobel Women" carried sand on horseback from the South River valley some miles to the east.

On June 2, 1755, John Berrisford, Robert Houston, and Daniel Lyle gave their bond of 'one hundred and fifty pounds, current money of Virginia' to John Lyle, John Mackey, James Thompson, and Archibald Alexander for the construction of the building. They did their work well, with the assistance of the congregation so that the building was dedicated on October 3, 1756.

With Augusta Stone Church at fort Defiance, Timber Ridge is one of the two Colonial Presbyterian buildings in existence in Virginia.

General Samuel Houston, of Texas fame, was born in 1793 in the Houston home a short distance from the church where he worshipped and until his family moved to Tennessee when young Sam was fourteen.

GENERATION NINE

John McCroskey and Elizabeth Gay

John was born in 1680 in Wigtown, Ayrshire, Scotland and some sources say Antrim, Ireland was our first immigrant. He died in 1758 in Timber Ridge Virginia.   John's family immigrated in 1730 and settled on the Borden tract in Rock Bridge, VA.

John came to the U.S. in about 1735 apparently to Virginia settling near the Shenandoah Mountains, in about 1742. By tradition the family came from Wigtown in the southwest of the Scottish lowlands directly across from Ireland. They would have then moved to Northern Ireland in about 1680 where John was born. John McCroskey's family was closely associated with that of John Houston. John McCroskey with one full brother came with the Houstons from Virginia to Sevier and Blount Co.. Tenn., which was then part of North Carolina and there settled. The Houstons and McCroskeys intermarrying after they arrived in Tenn. or what was then known as the territory of Franklin, by which name the State was first called.

In 1753 John McCroskey was listed as a subscriber to the New Providence Church, which along with the congregation of Timber Ridge had united in a call to the Rev. John Brown.
Elizabeth Gay was born 1685 in Wigtown, Ayrshire, Scotland / OR Antrim, Ireland and died in 1758 in Rockbridge, VA.
Elizabeth's parents were John Gay and Mary Fisher. John Gay was from Ulster, Ireland and died in Dedham, Massachusetts.

John and Elizabeth's Children:

Elizabeth – 1730-1797married Samuel Cunningham Houston – her son was the famous Texan Sam Houston. Sam Houston was born on Borden's tract in Timber Ridge, Rockbridge VA and died in 1863 in Huntsville, Walker Texas.
Robert – 1712-
William 1714-1856 Ireland to Maryville, TN married Elizabeth McClearage
John 1715-1811 married Sarah Hays, children: Elizabeth, James, John, Joseph, Alexander, Andrew
Margaret 1718-1799 Ireland to VA married William Caruthers
Esther 1720-1758 in Antrim, Ireland to Virginia – married James Hope

James 1720-1782 Derry, Ireland to Augusta VA. Married Elizabeth Hayes
   Alexander 1722-1797
   David 1730-1788 Augusta, VA to Licking Kentucky. Married Grizel Poague.

Samuel Smith – 1725 married Elizabeth Blair

GENERATION TEN

John McCroskey and Louise McCroskey
John 1620 – Ireland to

Louisa 1600-1648 born and died in Scotland

BORDEN TRACT IN TIMBER RIDGE, VA – JOHN MCCROSKEY'S LAND

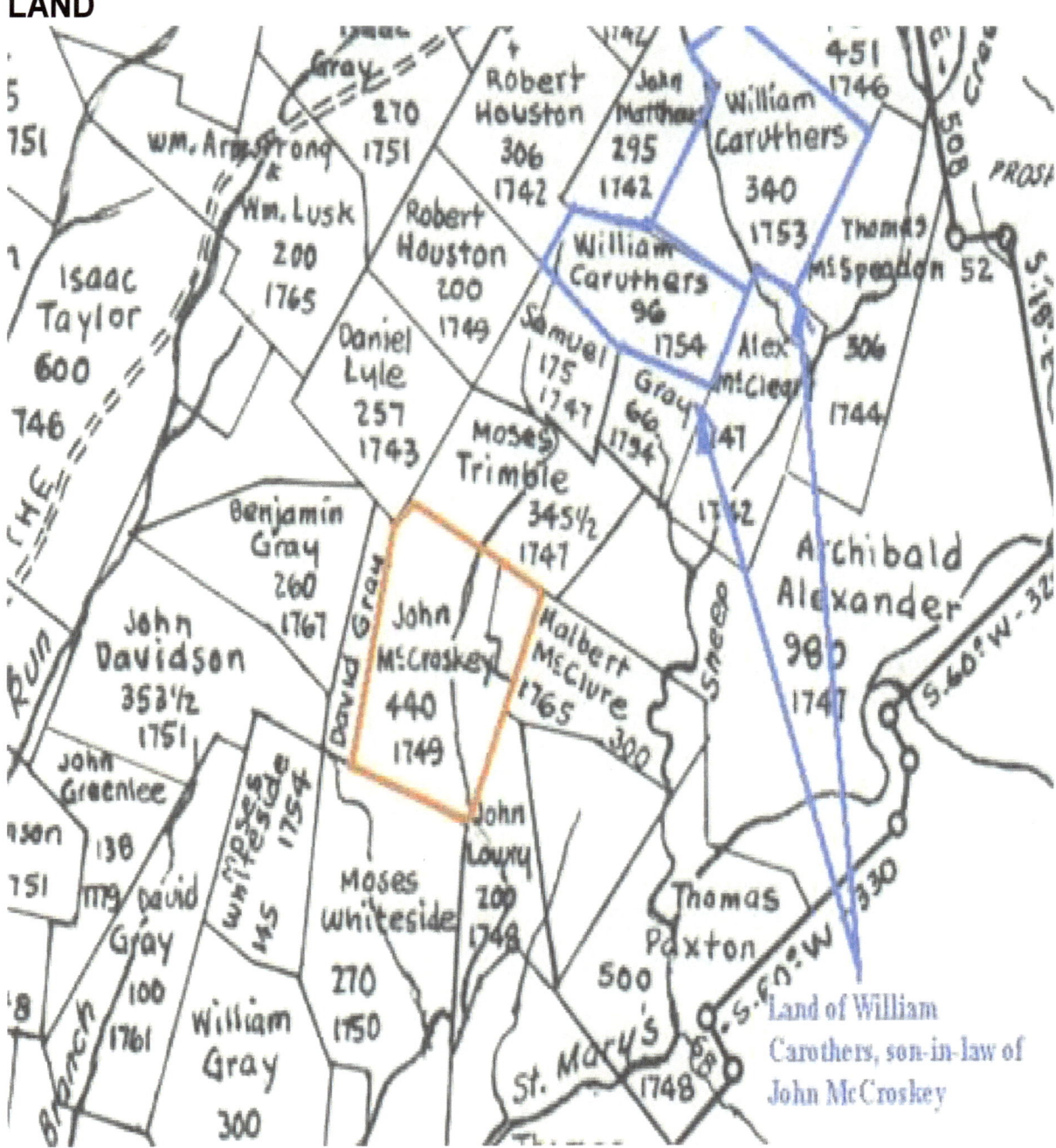

John's son John McCroskey was deposed in 1806 at age 90. He said the land when he first knew it was sixty years ago [1746], and was called Paxton's land. Thos. Taylor, son-in-law of Thos. Paxton, was the first settler.

JOHN'S WILL

The Will of the first John McCroskey, who died in 1758, in Augusta County, Virginia, and which is on file in the courthouse at Staunton, Virginia reads as follows:"IN THE NAME OF GOD AMEN on the sixth day of May in the year of our Lord 1758, L John McCroskf}' of the County of Augusta in the Collony of Virginia, Planter, being sick and weak of body but of perfect mind and memory, thanks be given unto Almighty God, therefore calling unto mind the mortality of my body and that it is appointed unto all men once to die, do make and ordain this, my last Will and Testament. That is to say principally and first of all I give and recommend my Soul into the hands of Almighty God that gave it, and for my body I recommend itto the Earth to be buried in a Christian like and decent manner at the descretion of my executors, nothing doubting but at the general Ressurection I shall receive the same again by the mighty power of God, and as touching such worldly Estate wherewith it hath pleased God to bless me in this life, I give, design, bequeath and dispose of the same in the following manner and form, and first I declare it is to be my will that all myjust debts that I owe and all my funeral charges be paid and satisfied.

Item: I give and bequeath unto my dearly beloved wife Elizabeth, her bed and furniture, being the best bed in the House while she lives, and at her death I order my daughter Elizabeth to get it if she be alive. I order my wife the third part of all my household plenishings and a brown horse branded on the near buttock-IE and slit in the near ear, and her saddle and bridle, and two cows, and all her clothes.

Item: I give unto my Son, James McCroskey ten shillings Current money o Virginia.

Item: I give unto my Son-in-Law, William Camrthers ten shillings.

Item: I give unto my Son, William McCroskey ten shillings.

Item: I give unto my Son-in-Law, Samuel Huston ten shillings.

Item: I give unto my Son, Alexander McCroskry ten shillings.

Item: I give unto my Son, Samuel McCroskry ten shillings.

Item: I give unto my Son, David McCroskry ten shillings.

Item: I give unto my Son-in-Law, James Hope ten shillings.

Item: I give unto my Grand-daughter, Margaret Hope seven pounds Virginia money to be paid her by the Executors in case she be alive, and if not to be given to her two brothers.

Item: I order that my two Sons, Samuel and David pay the five ten-pound bonds assigned by me to my two Sons James and William McCroskry in case they lose not their lands by the Enemy, but if they do they are not to pay the money.

Item: I give unto my two Sons James and William six pounds in Gold and six pounds in paper money to equably divided betwixt them.

Item: I give unto my wife Thomas Hills bond of Eight pounds. I order that the bond of Robert and Alexander Tedfords to pay Margret Hope the above mentioned seven Pounds.

Item: I give unto my Son-in-Law Samuel Huston a four pound Bond of my Son John.

I order that all my moveables with a bond of James and Isaac Andersons be equabbly divided betwixt my Sons and Daughters.

I do hereby constitute, ordain and appoint my Son Samuel McCroskey Andrew Hays, and Alexander Miller, Executors of this my last Will and Testament and I do utterly disallow, revoke and disannul all and other former Wills and Testaments legacies and Executors by me in any way before this time named willed and bequeathed notified and confirmed this and no other to be my Last Will and Testament in Witness whereof I have hereunto set my hand and Seal the day and year above written.

Signed, sealed, published, pronounced and declared by the and Testament in the presence of us the subscribers.

John Coskry (Seal)

LAND DEED RECORDS

Land, Marriage, and Probate Records, 1639-1850 Name: John McCroskey
Date: 21 Aug 1747
Location: Augusta Co., VA
Property: 306 acres, part of 92100 &c. on North Fork of the Creek; corner to William Buchanan; Isaac Anderson's line; James McDowell's land.
Notes: This land record was originally published in "Chronicles of the Scotch-Irish Settlement in Virginia, 1745-1800. Extracted from the Original Court Records of Augusta County" by Lyman Chalkley.
Remarks: Acknowledgement 21 Aug 1747. 9.9.2. Sold in testator Benj. Borden, Sr.'s lifetime. Grantor, Benj. Borden &c.
Description: Grantee
Book_Date: 1-363

Virginia Land, Marriage & Probate Records, 1639-1850
Name: John McCroskey
Date: 29 Aug 1750
Location: Augusta Co., VA
Property: 480 acres; corner John McCroskey and Isaac Anderson.
Notes: This land record was originally published in "Chronicles of the Scotch-Irish Settlement in Virginia, 1745-1800. Extracted from the Original Court Records of Augusta County" by Lyman Chalkley.
Description: Neighbor
Book_Date: 2-813

WILL OF JOHN MCCROSKEY, SON OF JOHN AND ELIZABETH GAY

John McCroskey, a son of John and Elizabeth (Gay) McCroskey, was born in County Antrim, Ireland September 26, 1715 and died in Rockbridge County VA in 1811. His will, dated June 18, 1808, is recorded on pages 354 and 355 of Will Book 3 in Rockbridge County VA. His will follows: "In the name of God amen I John McCroskey of the County of Rockbridge and the State of Virginia do make and appoint this to be my last Will and Testament in manner and form following Viz I do will that after my decease all my just debts shall be paid and that my worldly Estate whatever either real or personal which may remain shall be for the intire use and benefit and at the disposal of my son Joseph McCroskey during his natural life and at his decease it shall be equally divided amongst his children, excepting the sum of one dollar to each of my other children which I allow to be made paid unto them within one year after my decease if they chuse to call for it -- And I do Will and appoint my son Joseph McCroskey sole Executor of this my last Will and Testament, revoking and disannulling all former wills by me heretofore made and establishing and confirming this as my last Will and Testament-- In Testimony whereof I have hereunto set my hand and affixed my seal this tenth day of June in the year of our lord one thousand eight hundred and eight--

 John McCroskey [his mark] (seal)

Signed Sealed and acknowledged as the last Will & Testament in the presence of us

John Adams

Andw Findley

James Adams

At Rockbridge County Court July 1st 1811

A writing purporting to be the last Will & Testament of John McCroskey

deceased was produced in Court by Joseph McCroskey the executor

therein named and proved by the oath of John Adams, Andrew Findley and

James Adams Witnesses thereto and ordered to be Recorded-- And on the

motion of said Executor who made oath according to Law probate thereof

is granted him in due form on his giving Bond & Security and he together

with Andrew Findley & John Adams his securities entered into &

acknowledged Bond in the penalty of $5000 Conditioned according to Law

Sketches Of

Tennessee's Pioneer Baptist Preachers

ELIJAH ROGERS

(pages 425 - 429)

I am now standing on historic ground-the ancient site of the Forks of Little Pigeon (now Sevierville) Church, the first Baptist church of Sevier County, constituted in 1789. Just out there stood the old meeting-house, where the Baptist saints worshipped, and where Richard Wood and Elijah Rogers preached the gospel and ministered to them as pastors for more than fifty years. And here in the old cemetery is a tombstone bearing the inscription: "Sacred to the memory of Elijah Rogers; born May, 1774 ; died May, 1841."

Maj. E. E. McCroskey, a descendant of Elijah Rogers, says the Rogers family is originally from Wales. In its later history it was identified with the Puritan stock of Plymouth Rock fame. Two brothers of this name came from over the waters in the "May Flower" with the goodly company of the Pilgrim Fathers. One of them located in Massachusetts, the other in Virginia. The members of the family in the New England states have an unbroken family record back to the year 1300.

Elijah, the son of Henry Rogers, was born in Fauquier County, Virginia, but at the age of 15 came with his father and other members of the family to Sevier County, Tennessee, then a part of the "western territory" of North Carolina. This county at that early date was largely an unsubdued wilderness, infested by the Indians, whose hostile aggressions, for a number of years, involved the races in perpetual warfare or vigilant watching on the part of the settlers against the sudden raids of the hostile and suspecting natives. In all this young Rogers was an "active participant." (S. C. Rogers, in Borum's Sketches.)

Elijah Rogers lived before the day of public schools in Sevier County, or even private ones. But his battle with the wilderness developed in him strength of character as well as strength of muscle. He was in every sense a self-made man. His education, from first to last, was secured by hard digging and persistent application. He possessed the talent of self I helpfulness and acquired in large measure the virtue of self reliance. In his early ministry and even on toward middle life, though not lacking in masculine strength, he was "raw and awkward and unpromising," we are told; yet by dint of effort and perseverance he became, in time, a fairly polished speaker, for his day.

At the age of 20 Elijah Rogers was married to Miss Katherine Clack, daughter of Spencer Clack, a Baptist, and a prominent citizen of Sevier County-one of a delegation of "five members," elected to represent his county in a convention called by the Governor (William Blount) to meet at Knoxville, January 11, 1796, to formulate the first constitution for the government of the new State of Tennessee (Ramsey's Annals, p. 651) ; and was also a member of the legislature for a number of terms. This union was blessed with a family of ten children, five sons and five daughters.

In 1796 he and his companion united with the Forks of Little Pigeon (Sevierville) Church, and were baptized, it is supposed, by Elder Richard Wood, who was then pastor of the church. Subsequently this church licensed him to preach, but he was not ordained to the full work of the ministry till he had reached his thirty-sixth year.

In 1810 Boyd's Creek Church called for his ordination, and he was accordingly ordained, in the usual way, as we may suppose, by the laying on of the hands of a presbytery, presumably by the authority of the old Forks of Little Pigeon Church, of which he seems still to have been a member.

He served Boyd's Creek, Alder Branch, and Sevierville as pastor the greater part of his ministerial life. Of Boyd's Creek he was pastor more than thirty years. He was the first pastor of Alder Branch, he and Augustine Bowers being the joint founders of the church. He was successor to Elder Richard Wood in the pastorate of the Sevierville Church. For more than fifty-two years these two faithful under-shepherds took care of the Baptist flock at Sevierville, each serving the flock faithfully to the close of his life.

These men were present at the baptism of John Hillsman (August, 1825) in the Tennessee River at Knoxville, in the presence of 3,000 people, Elijah Rogers being the administrator. This was the first baptism in the city of Knoxville, and the beginning of Baptist history at this now Baptist city. (Old record.)

These two men were the chief pillars of strength to the Baptist cause in all their part of the country for years, serving the churches, for the most part, at their own charge. They, with other Baptists, had seen and felt the injustice of a compulsory religious (?) tax to support the state church, and the pendulum had swung the other way. Right or wrong, following the Baptist custom of the times, they said little about pastoral support, and "farmed" for a living. "Preacher Rogers" was held in repute as a farmer, and was said to be the "best corn-grower" in Sevier County.

Elijah Rogers was moderator of the Tennessee Association twenty-four years in succession - a fact in itself showing unusual influence and popularity, and an honor rarely duplicated in the history of deliberative bodies.

He was pioneer in missions, and a John the Baptist preparing the way for a missionary movement, even while he was held in fellowship by his anti-mission and anti-effort brethren. While the leaders of the anti-mission school gave their time and energy to discussing "fixed fate, free-will and foreknowledge absolute," Elijah Rogers was one of the first to break the shell of fatalistic belief and declare for missions. His contention was for "free salvation," or a salvation available for all men, a universal commission, and the obligation of the churches to give the "gospel to every creature." In the war with the so-called "Ironsides" he was able and distinguished as a fighter. He had an appointment, I am told, on one occasion between the "missionaries" and the "antis." The appointed day came round, the multitude gathered, the sermon - a "great sermon" - was preached. It was a great triumph for the cause of truth. The opposition was not entirely quieted, but to a great extent was disarmed. The friends of missions were encouraged, and furnished arguments for the defense of their cause. The controversial spirit, however, was not natural to him. He was inclined to be conservative and conciliatory, rather than combative. Churches, rent asunder by strife over the question of missions, sent for Elder Rogers, far and near, to help them settle their troubles; and few men could do more by tact and prudence than he to restore peace and unity to a divided church.

I close the sketch with the relation of the following anecdote, which is vouched for by good authority. Elder Rogers had a small Testament which he was accustomed to carry about with him in one of the hind pockets of his coat.

While getting ready to start to one of his Saturday appointments he happened upon a pack of cards about the barn, which some of his boys, as he supposed, had been playing on the sly, and had forgotten to "hide", as they intended to do.

He put the cards in the same pocket in which he had previously put his Testament, and went on to church, intending to give the boys a lecture, on his return home. When the time to begin the preaching service had arrived, he had forgotten all about the "cards". Imagine his surprise, when, putting his hand in his pocket for his Testament, he pulled out the cards instead, in plain view of the audience. As soon, however, as he could recover himself from his embarrassing perplexity, he explained the situation and proceeded to give a moral lecture on the wickedness and folly of "card-playing".

Burnett, J .J. Sketches of Tennessee's Pioneer Baptist Preachers. Nashville, Tenn.: Press of Marshall & Bruce Company, 1919.

URL: http://www.knoxcotn.org/tnbap tists/index.html

OTHER BOOKS BY KATHERINE FLETCHER

Can be ordered on Amazon as paperback and/or Kindle

The Rice Family History – Ireland to West Tennessee

The Turnage Family History – Essex, England to W. Tennessee

England, McKinney & Little family history – West Tennessee branch

Trent Family History – East Tennessee Branch

Natural Stress Busters

Real Treasure Hunting for Beginners: Finding Fossil, Rocks, Artifacts

Children's books:

Why do People Eat?

What Happens When We Die?

YOUR OWN FAMILY NOTES

YOUR OWN FAMILY NOTES

YOUR OWN FAMILY NOTES

YOUR OWN FAMILY NOTES

YOUR OWN FAMILY NOTES